Cool
Sports Parties

Perfect Party Planning for Kids

Karen Latchana Kenney

A Division of ABDO
ABDO
Publishing Company

visit us at www.abdopublishing.com

Published by ABDO Publishing Company, a division of ABDO, P.O. Box 398166, Minneapolis, Minnesota 55439. Copyright © 2012 by Abdo Consulting Group, Inc. International copyrights reserved in all countries. No part of this book may be reproduced in any form without written permission from the publisher. Checkerboard Library™ is a trademark and logo of ABDO Publishing Company.

Printed in the United States of America, North Mankato, Minnesota
052011
092011

 PRINTED ON RECYCLED PAPER

Interior Design and Production: Colleen Dolphin, Mighty Media, Inc.
Cover Design: Aaron DeYoe
Series Editor: Liz Salzmann
Photo Credits: Colleen Dolphin, Shutterstock

The following manufacturers/names appearing in this book are trademarks:
Aleene's® Original Tacky Glue®, Elmer's® Glue-All®, FabricMate® Markers, Lunds & Byerly's® Whole Milk, Morton® Salt, Proctor Silex® Hand Mixer, Sharpie® Fine Point Marker, Sharpie® Paint Markers

Library of Congress Cataloging-in-Publication Data

Kenney, Karen Latchana.
  Cool sports parties : perfect party planning for kids / Karen Latchana Kenney.
      p. cm. -- (Cool parties)
  Includes index.
  ISBN 978-1-61714-977-1
  1. Children's parties--Planning--Juvenile literature. 2. Sports--Juvenile literature. I. Title.
  GV1205.K473 2012
  793.2'1--dc22
                          2011004214

Contents

It's Sports Party Time! 4

Party Planning Basics 6

What's Your Theme? 8

Tools & Supplies 10

Invitations
Flying Soccer Ball Invite 12

Decorations
Bowling Ball & Pin Door Curtain 14

Party Favors
Personalized Water Bottles 16

Party Food
What's on the Menu? 18

Sample Party Menus 20

Touchdown Taters 22

Party Activities
Gnarly Board T-shirt 24

Sporty Race Car Frames 26

Martial Arts Headband 28

Conclusion 30

Glossary 31

Web Sites 31

Index 32

It's Sports Party Time!

It's fun to shoot hoops and try skateboarding tricks, isn't it? Hosting a sports party is one great way to play those sports with your friends! Pick your favorite sport to play at your party. Then plan games and activities based on that sport. It will be a blast!

But to make this party happen, you need to plan out the **details**. Start with the basics, like the *when* and *where* of the party. Then move on to details like decorations and **menus**. Create some cool invitations and send them out. And don't forget to plan the activities! They keep the party moving at a fun pace.

Remember to plan and do as much as you can before the party starts. It takes time and hard work to be a host. But it's definitely worth it! Then all that's left for you to do is have fun!

Safety

- Ask for an adult's help when making food for your party.

- Find out where you can make crafts and play games. Do you need to protect a table surface? What should you use?

- Check the party room. Can anything be broken easily? Ask a parent to remove it before the party.

- Should guests bring any sports safety gear to the party? Remind them in the invitation.

Permission

- Do you have space at your house where you can play your sport? Or will you need to go to a park or rec center?

- How much money can you spend? Where can you shop and who will take you?

- Make sure guests' parents know who will be overseeing the party.

- Can you put up decorations? How?

- How long should the party last? When should guests go home?

- Talk about who will clean up after the party.

Party Planning Basics

Every great party has the same basic **details**. They are the *who*, *what*, *when*, and *where* of the party. Your party planning should begin with these basics. Then make lists of everything you need to buy, make, and do for the party. You should also have a list of everyone you invited. Mark whether each guest can come or not.

Who: How many friends do you want to invite? And who will they be? Try to pick friends who will get along and have fun.

What: What is the sports party for? Is it your birthday? Or just for fun? You'll need to explain this on the invitation.

When: Parties are best on the weekends. Pick a Saturday or Sunday. But, don't plan the party on a weekend with a holiday.

Where: Is the party at your house, at a park, or at a party room? Explain the details to your guests. And, don't forget to include directions!

Favors:

What to buy:

What to make:

Activities:

What to buy:

What to make:

Menu:

Decorations:

What to buy:

What to make:

Music:

Equipment:

Guests:

_____ yes/no

_____ yes/no

_____ yes/no

_____ yes/no

_____ yes/no

_____ yes/no

What's Your Theme?

What sports do you like to play? Select one and make it your party theme. Use your favorite basketball team colors to decorate. Or assemble your own bowling pins from water bottles and marbles!

Once you've chosen a sport, plan all the **details** around that theme. From food to favors and invitations to games, the party details can relate to the sport you chose. Using a theme makes all the elements of your party go together. Check out the party themes on the next page. There are activities in this book to match each one.

Soccer

Kick the ball down the field. But don't use your arms or hands! See how many goals you can score!

Football

Are you a quarterback or a defensive linesman? Whatever your position, football is about making touchdowns!

Basketball

Free throws and slam dunks make basketball fun. Play one-on-one or on teams. Test your skills on the court!

Bowling

How many pins can you knock down? It takes skill to roll the ball down the lane. Remember to wear bowling shoes!

Car Racing

Fast cars, race tracks, and cheering fans make car races entertaining. Play with remote-controlled race cars. Then talk about your favorite race car drivers!

Martial Arts

Do you have a white belt or a black belt? Practice your kicks, punches, and blocks. Show your friends your moves!

Skateboarding

Can you do an Ollie or a Kickflip? Get together at a skate park. Or use ramps in your backyard.

Don't forget...

After you pick your theme, let guests know all about it. Do they need to bring something or wear special clothes? Let them know on the invitation. That way guests will show up prepared. They'll also be even more excited to party!

Tools & Supplies

Here are some of the things you'll need to do the activities in this book:

pepper

shredded cheese

chopped chives

oven mitts

salt

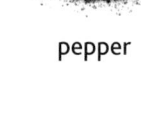
paper plates

freezer paper

olive oil

red potatoes

measuring cups

mixing bowls

baking sheet

mixer

milk

measuring spoons

sour cream

butter

white cotton T-shirt

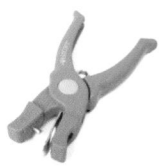
hole punch

plain wood frames

paint pens,
medium or fine tip

white A2 folded cards

glue stick

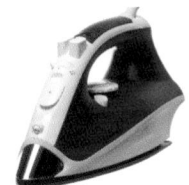
iron

newspaper

markers

foam adhesive
letters and shapes

mosaic tiles,
black and white

white canvas fabric

white streamers

construction paper

fabric markers

stainless steel
water bottles

craft glue

tape measure

stickers

Flying Soccer Ball Invite

Your friends will think this invite is kickin'!

Let's Play Soccer

Let's Play Soccer!

SoccerTheme

1 Cut a half circle out of yellow paper to make a sun. Glue the sun to the card. The flat edge of the sun should line up with the folded edge of the card.

2 Cut a light green and a dark green strip of paper. They should be 5½ x 1 inches (14 x 3 cm). Then cut a **jagged** edge on each strip. Now they look like grass.

3 Glue one grass strip ½ inch up from the bottom of the card. Glue the second grass strip with the edge lined up with the bottom of the card.

4 Put a foam adhesive dot close to the grass. Stick a soccer ball sticker onto the dot. Use a marker to draw motion lines on one side of the ball. Make it look like the ball is flying through the air!

5 Write "Let's Play Soccer!" along the bottom of the sun. Open the card and write the party **details** inside.

More Ideas!

SKATEBOARDING THEME
Cut card stock into the shape of a skateboard. Draw a cool **design** on the front. Write the party details on the back.

CAR RACING THEME
Draw a racetrack on the card. Cut car shapes out of colored paper. Glue them on the track. Add some motion lines. Write the party details inside the card.

MARTIAL ARTS THEME
Make karate belt invitations that guests can wear to the party. Cut long strips of **fabric**. Write the party details on them with a fabric pen.

13

Bowling Ball & Pin Curtain

Guests will know they're at the right house!

What You Need

- drinking glass
- black construction paper
- pencil
- scissors
- white construction paper
- hole punch
- glue
- red marker
- white streamers
- tape

14

Bowling Theme

1 Put the glass upside down on the black paper. Trace around it with the pencil. Draw 24 circles and cut them out. These are the bowling balls.

2 Punch the white paper with a hole punch 72 times. Save the dots. Glue three dots in a triangle near the edge of each ball.

3 Draw a bowling pin shape on white paper. It should be about the same size as the bowling balls. Cut it out and use it to trace 23 more pins. Cut out the rest of the pins. Use the red marker to draw two red stripes on the neck of each pin. The stripes should curve slightly.

4 Cut eight pieces of streamer. They should be almost as long as the door is tall.

5 Glue six balls or six pins to each streamer. Space them out evenly. Tape the top of each streamer to the top of the doorway. **Alternate** the bowling pin and bowling ball streamers.

More Ideas!

FOOTBALL THEME
Select paper in the colors of your favorite football team. Cut triangles from the paper. Then glue them to string to make a **pennant** banner.

CAR RACING THEME
Use black marker to color checkerboards on white paper. Then glue them to wooden dowels to make flags. Stick the flags around the party room.

BASKETBALL THEME
Blow up balloons in your favorite basketball team's colors. Stick **skewers** through the knots. Put the skewers in a vase to make a balloon **bouquet**.

Personalized Water Bottles

What You Need

newspaper

stainless steel water bottles

paint pens, medium or fine tip

These water bottles make great party favors!

Basketball Theme

1 Protect the table with newspapers. Then position the water bottle sideways on the table.

2 Use an orange paint pen to draw a basketball. Place it near the top of the water bottle. Draw an orange circle and color it in.

3 While the basketball dries, write a guest's name on the bottle with a colored paint pen. Start near the bottom and move up to the ball. Make the letters thick and big. If it's a long name, write it above or below the ball.

4 While the letters dry, use a black paint pen to outline the circle. Then draw two straight lines across the circle. Add a half circle on each side of the ball.

5 Finish by outlining the letters in black. Then let it dry completely before touching the paint. Make a water bottle for each guest!

More Ideas!

FOOTBALL THEME
Make foam football pins. Cut football shapes out of foam. Tape a safety pin to the back of each foam football. These pins are great to put on backpacks!

SOCCER THEME
Make soccer ball magnets. Glue a clear, flat marble to the front of a soccer ball picture. The picture should be the same size as the marble. Glue a button magnet to the back.

CAR RACING THEME
Create race car driver's **licenses** for your guests using card stock. Think of a cool racing name for each guest. Cover the cards with clear contact paper.

What's on the Menu?

A great party isn't complete without delicious snacks and cool drinks! It's best to make finger foods. They are fun to eat and easy to carry. Everyone can still mingle while they snack. To plan your party **menu**, think about a few things first.

Variety

Everyone has different tastes. Make sure you have some sweet and some salty things. Have healthy choices and **vegetarian** dishes too.

Meals

Will your party last a long time? You will need more than just snacks if it does. Think about the time of day when your party will take place. Will your guests need breakfast, lunch, or dinner? And maybe they'll want snacks too!

Amount

How many people are coming? Plan to have enough food to feed everyone.

Time

It takes time to shop for and prepare food. Pick recipes that you have time to make. Remember, there are other things you need to do before the party.

Allergies

Check with your guests to see if they have any food **allergies**. Make sure there are things those guests can eat.

Sample Party Menus

It's fun to plan your menu around your party theme. Here are some examples.

Black Belt Martial Arts Menu

Karate "Chopped" Salad Wraps

Mini Egg Rolls

Sesame Chicken Skewers

Fortune Cookies

Spicy Ginger Ale

Kick Off Football Menu

Touchdown Taters*
*recipe on page 22!

Zesty Buffalo Wings

Raw Veggies & Dip

Chocolatey Chip Bars

Hot Apple Cider

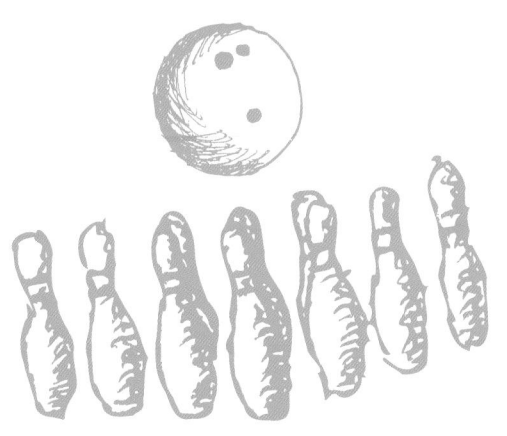

Hit the Lanes Bowling Menu

Sky High Sub Sandwiches

Grilled Veggie Nachos

Pretzel & Peanut Snack Mix

Black & White Marble Cake

Very Vanilla Milk Shakes

Slam Dunk Basketball Menu

Free-throw Fruit Salad Cups

Cheese Ball and Crackers

Mini Turkey Burgers

Carrot Cake Cupcakes

Orange Fizz Punch

Ask for help finding easy and delicious recipes to make.

Touchdown Taters

Scoring touchdowns creates mean appetites!

What You Need

24 small red potatoes
baking sheet
measuring cups
½ cup olive oil
salt and pepper
oven mitts
knife
spoon
mixing bowl
measuring spoons
¼ cup milk
½ stick butter
¼ cup sour cream
mixer
½ cup shredded cheddar or
    colby cheese
¼ cup chopped chives

Football Theme

1 Set the oven to 350 degrees. Then wash and dry the potatoes. Put them on the baking sheet and sprinkle them with the olive oil and a little salt and pepper.

2 Ask an adult to help you put the potatoes in the oven. Bake them for 45 minutes. See if they are done by poking them with a sharp knife. If it slides in easily, the potatoes are done.

3 Take the potatoes out of the oven. Let them cool enough to touch without burning yourself.

4 Cut off the tops of the potatoes. Scoop out the insides of each potato. Leave about ½ inch of potato next to the skins.

5 Put the potato tops and insides in the mixing bowl. Add the milk, butter, sour cream, and ½ teaspoon each of salt and pepper. Mix until the ingredients are combined but still lumpy.

6 Put the potatoes back on the baking sheet. Spoon the filling into the potatoes. Put some of the shredded cheese on each one. Bake them in the oven for 5 minutes, or until the cheese is melted.

7 Remove the potatoes from the oven. Sprinkle them with the chives. Serve the potatoes while they are still warm.

Gnarly Board T-Shirt

Paint a cool skateboard on a T-shirt!

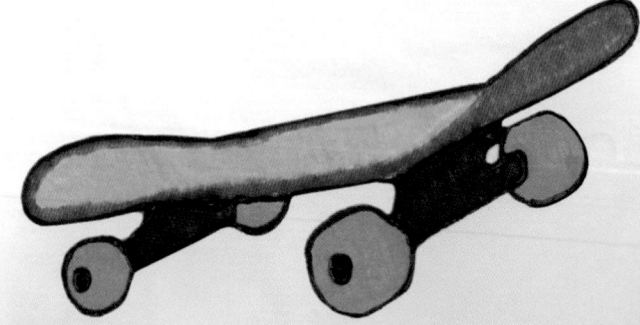

Skateboard Theme

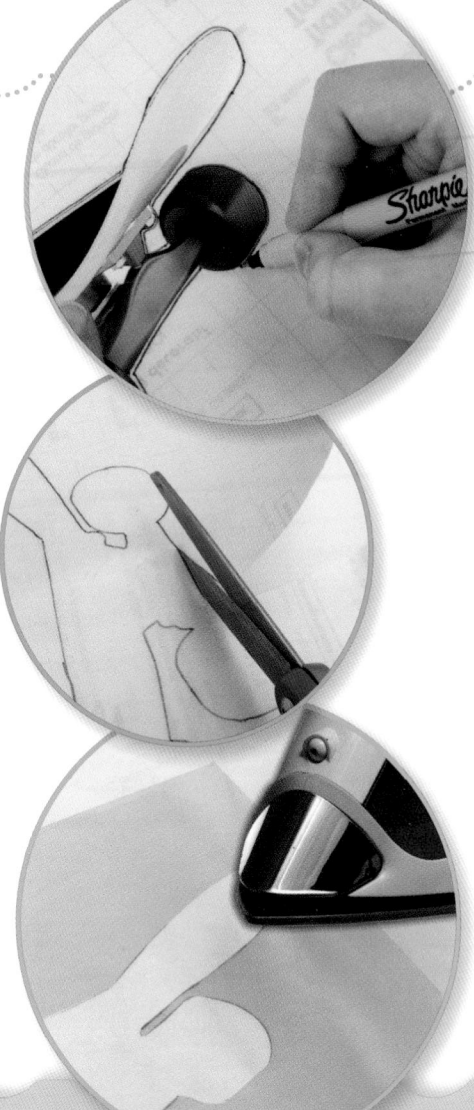

1 Before the party, wash and dry the shirts. This keeps them from **shrinking** later.

2 Cut a picture of a skateboard out of a magazine. Or you could draw one on paper and cut it out.

3 Cut a piece of freezer paper the same size as the front of a T-shirt. Trace the skateboard shape in the middle of the freezer paper on the non-waxy side.

4 Cut it out to make a skateboard-shaped hole in the freezer paper. Make one for each guest.

5 Iron one of the sheets of freezer paper to the front of each shirt. Make sure the waxy side is touching the **fabric**. Each shirt will have a skateboard **stencil** on it.

6 At the party, cover the table with newspaper. Set out the paint pens and fabric markers. Give each guest a T-shirt. Have them paint their skateboards. When the paint is dry, tear off the freezer paper.

More Ideas!

BOWLING THEME
Create your own bowling sets. Fill the bottoms of plastic bottles with marbles to make pins. Then use a rubber ball to knock them down.

SOCCER THEME
Make a soccer ball pencil topper. Use black and white modeling clay to make little soccer balls. Then stick them on the ends of pencils.

FOOTBALL THEME
Make foam football visors. Paint your name on a plain foam visor. Then add a few footballs or the name of your favorite team.

Sporty Race Car Frames

A checkered pattern is perfect for this frame!

What You Need

newspaper
plain wood frames
craft glue
paper plates
mosaic tiles,
  black and white
small foam letters
race car stickers

Car Racing Theme

1 Before the party, remove the glass from the frames. Cover the table with newspaper.

2 Give each guest a frame and a paper plate with glue on it. Tell everyone to dip one side of a black tile in the glue. Have them stick their tiles to a corner of their frames. Then they should glue a white tile next to the black tile. Have them **alternate** black and white tiles all around their frames.

3 After the glue dries, everyone can decorate their frames. Suggest they use foam letters to spell a fun racing term. And they can add race car stickers.

4 When the frames are dry, put the glass back into each frame. Then your guests can take their frames home!

More Ideas!

SKATEBOARDING THEME
Select cool pictures from skateboarding magazines and cut them out. Then stick them to your skateboard with clear contact paper.

BASKETBALL THEME
Make polymer clay basketballs. Use wire to make small rings. Stick one into each basketball before baking them. Then connect them to key chains.

MARTIAL ARTS THEME
Cut ninja stars out of cardboard. Hang up a large ring. Try to throw the stars through the ring. See who makes it the most.

Martial Arts Headband

Wear this headband with pride!

What You Need

- computer with Internet access
- white canvas fabric
- fabric markers
- scissors
- tape measure
- paper
- newspaper

Martial Arts Theme

亮 **bright**

1. Before the party, use the Internet to look up Chinese characters for different words. Try looking up words that **describe** people, like *strong* or *funny*. Print out the characters and English words, or write them down.

2. Cut strips of **fabric** for headbands. Make them 3 feet (1 m) long and 2 inches (5 cm) wide.

3. At the party, cover the table with newspaper. Set out the markers and the printouts of Chinese characters. Give each guest a headband.

4. Have your guests choose words that describe them. Then they can copy the Chinese characters for the words onto their headbands. The characters can go in the middle of the headband or at the ends. Have your guests add their names if they want.

5. Then everyone can wear their headbands! Just tie them on with the knot at the back.

More Ideas!

SOCCER THEME
Make tie-dyed soccer socks. Wrap rubber bands around different parts of the socks. Color them with permanent markers. Spray them with rubbing alcohol. Let the socks dry.

SKATEBOARD THEME
Do you know your skateboarding **lingo**? Write terms such as "the McTwist" on cards. Put the meanings on the backs of the cards. Then see who can get the most right!

BOWLING THEME
Turn T-shirts into bowling shirts. Paint a ball and pins on the back. On the front, write a number and your last name.

Conclusion

What a great sports party! Fun crafts! Good food! But, the party room is a mess! There's still work to do. Make sure you clean up and put everything back in order. Your parents will see what a responsible party host you are.

Was it your birthday? Did you keep track of your gifts? It's important to write down who gave you what. That will make sending thank-you cards easier. Make thank-you cards that match the party's theme. Write something **unique** and personal on each guest's card. It will make your friends feel special. Then send out the cards within a week after the party.

Hosting a party is hard work! There are so many **details** to plan and things to make. In the end, though, it all comes together to make a party to remember! Sports parties are fun, but what will your next party be? Check out the other books in the *Cool Parties* series for great ideas.

Glossary

allergy – sickness caused by touching, breathing, or eating certain things.

alternate – to change back and forth from one to the other.

bouquet – a bunch of flowers gathered together or arranged in a vase.

describe – to tell about something with words or pictures.

design – a decorative pattern or arrangement.

detail – a small part of something.

fabric – woven material or cloth.

jagged – pointy or uneven.

license – an official card or form that says you are allowed to do a particular thing.

lingo – special words or terms used for a particular job, sport, or activity.

menu – a list of things to choose from.

pennant – a triangular flag that often has a school or team logo on it.

shrink – to become smaller.

skewer – a long, thin, wood or metal stick with a sharp end.

stencil – a flat piece of paper, plastic, or metal with a shape cut out of it. It is used for tracing or painting the design onto another surface.

unique – different, unusual, or special.

vegetarian – without any meat.

Web Sites

To learn more about cool parties, visit ABDO Publishing Company on the World Wide Web at **www.abdopublishing.com**. Web sites about cool parties are featured on our book links page. These links are routinely monitored and updated to provide the most current information available.

Index

A

Activities and crafts
    doing, 24–25, 26–27, 28–29
    planning, 4, 5, 8–9
Adult help, for safety, 5, 23
Allergies, to foods, 19

B

Basic details, planning, 4, 5, 6–7
Basketball theme party,
    9, 15, 16–17, 21, 27
Bowling theme party,
    9, 14–15, 21, 25, 29

C

Car racing theme party,
    9, 13, 15, 17, 26–27
Cleaning up, 5, 30
Cost, 5

D

Decorations
    making, 14–15
    planning, 4, 5, 8–9

F

Favors
    making, 16–17
    planning, 8–9

Food

Food
    planning, 4, 18–19
    recipes, 22–23
    sample menus, 20–21
Football theme party,
    9, 15, 17, 20, 22–23, 25

G

Guest list, 6, 7
Guests, responsibilities of, 5, 9

H

Hosts, responsibilities of, 4, 30

I

Invitations
    making, 12–13
    planning, 4, 9

L

Lists, for planning, 6–7

M

Martial arts theme party,
    9, 13, 20, 27, 28–29
Menu
    planning, 4, 18–19
    samples, 20–21

P

Permission, for planning
    and hosting, 5
Potato snacks, recipe for, 22–23

S

Safety, 5
Skateboarding theme party,
    9, 13, 24–25, 27, 29
Soccer theme party,
    9, 12–13, 17, 25, 29

T

Thank-you cards, 30
Themes, choosing and planning,
    4, 6, 8–9
Tools and supplies, 10–11